Cash!

What would and should you do if you found a fortune?

Suzanne Visser

C_M_P

Clear Mind Press

CONTENTS

CONTENTS

Cash!
© Suzanne Visser
Published by Clear Mind Press, 2024
Alice Springs, Australia

ISBN Print: 978-0-6458887-4-4
Ebook; 978-0-6458887-5-1
Cover front: Suzanne Visser
Cover back: Suzanne Visser
Portrait of the Author: Hazel Blake

All inquiries should be made to the publisher: info@clearmindpress.com

https://www.clearmindpress.com

For M, who accidentally gave away the book to an op shop and then could not remember the title, nor the author. She only knew the book had a green and yellow cover and that it was a story about a girl who found cash in a tree. She wanted to reread it so badly, but she never found it again.

Day 1: Walking the Dog

I was not far from town, walking my dog, Red, in a nondescript piece of arid land next to the road leading to Hermannsburg. "Walking the dog" is an overstatement. I was sitting in the car while Red explored a piece of nondescript dirt at the side of the road. It was too hot to walk a dog that day. Going out had been a mistake. There was not a soul around. I had stopped the car and opened the door for Red. He had run into the patch of arid land that ended abruptly against the steep, red, rocky wall of West MacDonnell Ranges. There were rocks strewn everywhere, small trees, mulga scrubs and one big gum tree. Everything was shimmering in the stark afternoon light. I felt bored. Red peed against the white trunk of the ghost gum and then took a dump in the shade of its canopy. He looked ridiculous; staring into space while the turds left his bum. He stretched his whole body before he began to feverishly move his hind legs to bury the load he'd just lost. I laughed soundlessly. I expected him to return to the car, but there was something on the ground that demanded his attention. I called him.

"Red, come here!"

He looked up for a second but turned back to what he was exploring on the ground.

"Red! Come on!"

He did not even lift his big boof head. He was like that sometimes. He knew very well I was calling him but decided to not listen. It did not happen very often. When he was that way, I had to put him on the leash and kind of drag him. I dreaded getting out of the air-conditioned car into the prickly patch, but he left me no choice. He had his staffie-bum turned towards me now and his tail was wagging hard. I was worried that he would hurt his paws on hot rocks; burn the tender pillows that formed the bottom of his feet. I grabbed his leash from the back seat and tried one more time.

"Red, come here!"

He wagged his tail even more furiously, but he did not even lift his head. I sighed and reluctantly left the cool car. Immediately, a wall of heat slammed into me. Red was further away than I had estimated. I counted my steps to bear penetrating the heat.

Eighty, eighty-one, eighty-two...

"For heaven's sake, Red, come here."

He was sniffing at something. Not a half-rotten cadaver, I hoped; a bird or a rabbit... He would roll in it for sure and stink for a week. I tried to wade through the heat a little faster.

Hundred and thirty-one, hundred and thirty-two...

I wanted to reach him before he would start rolling. My linen dress was sticking around my body. Sweat was running down my sides. I was trying to avoid getting stones or prickles in my sandals. I was nearly tiptoeing.

Two-hundred and fifty-four, two-hundred and fifty-five....

There was not a breath of wind. I stepped into the shade of the gum tree. It turned out that Red was intensely sniffing the end of a limb of the gum tree that had snapped off. I hooked his leash onto his collar.

"Come on now. What's with the branch anyway."

Red refused to remove his nose from the branch.

Desperate to be out of the heat, I picked up the branch and carried it to the car. It was eaten by bugs inside. It was light. I lured Red into the car with it, then put it into the booth of the car for some reason. It stayed there, in the booth, for four days. Then I needed the booth.

2 |

Day 4: The Find

I had planned to take bags with old fabrics to the tip shop. I had not touched a sewing machine in years. I opened the trunk and saw something sticking from the end of the branch that was still in there. It looked man-made, a small roll of paper. I pulled it. Out came a roll of fresh green hundred-dollar bills tightly wrapped in a small sheet of brown paper that was glued tightly around the bills.

"Holy Christ!"
I quickly lowered my hand that held the money into the trunk and looked around.

Has anyone seen me?

The street was deserted. I stuffed the roll back into the branch, propped the branch under my arm, covered the end with my hand, and walked to the front door of my house quickly, Red in my wake as always.

"No, Red, you stay outside."

I put the branch on the dinner table in the living room. It was about a metre and a half long. I walked back to the door to make sure it was locked. I was not sure why. Red was in the yard, and nobody crossed Red. I never locked my door when home. Back at the table, I removed the roll of cash. It was rolled up so tightly that it was difficult to unroll. The bills sprang back into their rolled position when freed. I spread the green cylinders out over the table. One by one, I smoothed them on the rim of the tabletop against the direction of their spring. Once they were more or less flat, I stacked them. This took quite some time. I felt unreal. Here I was, suddenly unrolling hundred-dollar bills as if they were my own. Only they weren't mine. Were they?

I fetched the iron. Set on "wool" the bills were not at risk of getting burned. I added a rag for extra safety. After I had ironed the whole pile of hundred-dollar bills, I began to count. There were ninety-nine bills, totalling a whopping nine thousand and nine hundred dollars.

I looked around. What should I do with it? Take it to the bank? I looked at the pile and felt I had no right to even look at it. I fetched a heavy cast-iron grass-green casserole from the drying rack in the kitchen and placed it on the stack. Then I peered into the end of the branch. There was another roll sitting just behind where the first one had been!

What? Unbelievable!

I looked around for a tool to retrieve it. I remembered there was a small saw on top of the cupboard in the bedroom. I sawed the tip of the branch off while holding it pinched to a chair with my foot. With my thumb and index finger, I wiggled the roll free from the fresh wound in the wood. The roll was exactly the same size as the first one. I peered into the fresh wound. It smelled strongly of gum tree. About seven centimetres deep, there was another roll. And another one next to it. I turned the cast-iron casserole upside down and shoved the second roll underneath it. I put my foot on the branch on the chair. A small pile of sawdust gathered on the floor as I sawed another piece of the branch. The branch was considerably wider there. Two rolls of money were shaken free quite easily. I quickly put them under the casserole and looked around. I felt strongly as if I was doing something illegal. Was I?

When I had freed all twenty-two rolls from the branch's interior, I closed all curtains and began to iron the hundred-dollar bills. This gave me time to think, I told myself. But my thoughts were unruly and all over the place. I counted the hundred-dollar bills, stacked them, and placed the casserole over them. There was two hundred and seventy thousand and eight hundred dollars in total.

"Okay," I said, stupidly.

I then made a thinking sound: "Ehm."

My hands were moving strangely in front of me. I became mega-aware of myself and saw myself from the third person view: an older woman alone in a room talking to herself, gesturing. All the curtains are closed. There is an upside-down casserole on the table and a pile of sawdust on the floor. On a chair are pieces of a half rotten hollowed out gum wood. In a bin under the table are twenty-two pieces of brown paper. Under the casserole is two hundred and seventy thousand and eight hundred dollars. A scene from an arthouse movie.

Surreal!

"So, now what?" I said.

Should I go to the police? Should I hide the money?

This seemed like the best idea for now. I walked from room to room in the house looking for a safe place.

Should I tape the money under the top of my desk with duct tape?

I opened a drawer and checked if I had enough duct tape. There was a full spool of red linen tape. That would do the trick. But it was too obvious. Any thief would look there.

Am I scared of thieves now?

I had never been scared of or even concerned about thieves. I left my front door unlocked most of the time, when Red was in the yard anyway.

Am I a thief now?

I looked in the oven.

Nah, also too obvious.

What about the bed?

My bed was a wrought-iron affair with copper decorations. The corner poles were hollow. In the bedroom, I wiggled one copper lid free from the bedpost and peered inside. It was dark and hollow in there. I stood with the copper fixture in my hand, thinking.

Putting it in there is easy. But how do I get the money out of there again? I would have to destroy the bed. Should I bury the money in the garden then? No, too risky.

It was as if I were split into two persons having a heated conversation.

What about the kitchen bin? In the bottom with garbage on top?

No.

In the freezer then?

Everyone would put it in the freezer.

Take it with you?

Take it with me where? Am I going somewhere?

Yes, you are.

"Oh," I said surprised. I put the copper fixture back on the bedpost. It looked like the roof of a Russian church, I noticed.

Concentrate!

Leaving the money under the casserole on the table for now, locking the front door for a change, I walked along the meandering garden path to the gate.

"Come, Red, come on."

We walked to the car. I drove to the spot where Red had found the branch. I parked at the side of the road in the same place as before.

A man was standing in the shade of the ghost gum, looking around. There was no car in sight. How did he get there? What was he doing there? He seemed to look in my direction. He was too far to tell for sure. He was wearing sunglasses and an Akubra hat. I pretended to check my tyre and drove off, leaving Red disappointed and restless in the back seat.

"Now what?" I said again.

Not sure what to do next, I drove Red to the clay pans for a run. He was excited and frolicked like a dolphin in waves while I strolled in the heat waving the flies away from my face. Back at the car, I gave him a bowl of water that he lapped up sloppily. He fell asleep in the back seat, and I decided to go back to what I now thought of as The Spot. When I arrived, the man was gone. I put a fly net on and a hat and walked to the tree. Prickles were attacking my ankles and toes.

I should have changed my sandals for boots. Note to self for next time.

What next time?

I looked at the road towards Hermannsburg. No cars. I looked at the road toward town. Empty. I looked around on the ground. Were there any more white gum limbs? I saw a couple of thin branches but nothing one could hide anything in. I walked around the tree. Then I saw it: A dark hole at its bottom, there where the trunk disappeared into the ground.

"Jesus," I said and looked around again.

Like some sort of criminal.

Nobody! I squatted next to the trunk as if wanting to pee and stuck my hand in the hole. There were definitely more rolls in there. My hand closed around one. It shot towards me as if it was attached with an elastic band. At the same time, it was as if I moved in slow motion. I opened my hand. Yes, inside the brown paper were more green bills. I sat on my knees and dug into the hole with both hands.

An idiotic number of rolls came loose. I gathered them in the front of my dress that I held up like an apron. I ran to the car. It had been a while since I had run. But I ran smoothly, as if I had shed the past thirty years and the accompanying backache. I threw the loot on the passenger seat. Red opened one eye. I threw his blanket over the loot. I slammed the door shut and hurried to the driver's seat. The motor revved when I spurted away. Back home everything was as if I had left it.

Yes, duhuh, what did you expect?

I got two paper Woollies bags to carry the loot. The street shimmered, deserted in the sunlight.

3

Day 5: Ironing

The hundred-dollar bills were new. I was ironing them again at very low heat. Australian money was made of plastic. One couldn't scrunch it. It bounced back immediately. It was difficult to start a tear. I'd never paid much attention to what a hundred-dollar bill looked like, but now I got to know every inch of them. They feature detailed artwork and security features that celebrate significant aspects of the Australia's history and culture. The front had a portrait of Sir John Monash, a prominent Australian civil engineer and military commander during World War I. He was depicted in a formal pose, dressed in a suit and tie, radiating a dignified and authoritative presence. The background of the portrait included designs and patterns of Australian flora and fauna motifs and showed subtle security features like microprinting and fine lines. A vertical holographic strip ran alongside the portrait, displaying shifting images of the Australian Coat of Arms and a flying cockatoo when tilted. There was a transparent window that contained the Australian coat of arms and a stylised Federation Star. It was also embossed with a wave pattern that was tactile. Certain elements, such as the value numeral "100" and parts of the pattern, changed colour when viewed from different angles. The denomination "100" was prominently displayed at the top left and bottom right corners. The word "Australia" and "One Hundred Dollars" were also inscribed.

The reverse side featured a portrait of Dame Nellie Melba, one of Australia's most renowned opera singers. She was shown in formal attire that reflected her status. The background incorporated musical notes and scores intertwined with Australian native plant motifs, eucalyptus leaves and blossoms. A holographic strip was present on this side, displaying changing images when the bill was tilted. The transparent window on this side maintained the same security features as the front. Small, finely printed text that could only be read under magnification added another layer of security. The denomination "100" appeared again in the top left and bottom right corners. The text included "Australia" and "One Hundred Dollars". Certain parts of the note, such as the portraits and numerals, were printed with raised ink that could be felt when touched. Each bill had a serial number printed in two places. There was no way they were counterfeits.

After I had pressed, counted, and stacked all hundred-dollar bills, there was one million seventy-nine thousand one hundred dollars on the table. The stacks did not fit under the casserole any longer.

"What the hell is this?"

Bewildered, I fed Red and went to bed. I had not eaten dinner. While the adrenaline wore off, my muscles began to hurt.

4

Day 6: Fear

After a restless night full of half-dreams, I sat up in bed with a jolt. The door to the living room was open. I could see part of the dining table. It had not been a dream. The table was covered in green bills. Who did they belong to? A thief? And was I a thief for having taken them?

Should I turn myself in?

I stumbled out of bed and fed Red. Back inside, I made myself breakfast and sat at the table. There was no room for my plate and cup. I put them on top of the money. I laughed.

"Okay," I said again.

I must think through this methodically. What are my options? What does the law say about this?

"Screw the law," I said. A bold statement coming from a lawyer.

Nobody knows I've got the money.

What about the man?

The finders-keepers rule!

The finders-keepers rule suggested that whoever finds an object gets to keep it. The basic principle is that the finder of a lost item can claim ownership rights over it against everyone except the true owner. The rule was estqablished in Armory v Delamirie (1722). Parker v British Airways Board (1982) elaborated on it. It held that a finder of an item on another's property has rights to the item against all except the true owner, unless the property owner has manifested an intention to control the premises and the things on it. Each state and territory had specific legislation that could impact the rights of finders. For a finder to claim rights over a found item, they must: take possession of the item (I did), intend to exercise control over it (I did), and the finder must make reasonable efforts to locate the true owner (I did not). The finder may be required to notify the police or relevant authorities (I did not). Items found in public places generally follow the common law principle of finders-keepers against all except the true owner.

On my MacBook, I asked ChatGPT: "What does the law in Australia say about finding money?"

It answered: "Fnding a large sum of money and keeping it without making reasonable attempts to locate the owner can be considered theft or 'larceny by finding.' The law requires that you take steps to find the owner, such as handing the money over to the police. You are legally required to attempt to reunite the found money with its rightful owner. This includes handing it in to the police or using any identifiable information to try and locate the owner. If you keep the money without trying to find the owner, you could be charged with larceny. This offence is punishable by up to five years in prison if handled by the District Court. If dealt with in the Local Court, the maximum penalty for property valued over five-thousand dollars is two years imprisonment or a fine of eleven-hundred dollars. Actions considered reasonable to locate the owner include handing the money to the police or making inquiries based on any available information. If you hand the money over to the authorities and the owner is not found within a certain period (typically several months), you may be entitled to keep the money. However, this is handled on a case-by-case basis."

ChatGTP is a better lawyer than most human ones, better than I'll ever be.

I thought about the police and all the lawyers I knew in town. They'd probably keep the loot. No, I was not going to report it just yet. I could always report it later. I had to properly think about this first. I stuffed six thousand hundred dollars in one of the bedposts, in case I got caught. The question that followed logically now was: What are you going to do with it? This was a much more complicated question than one might expect. I sat at the table stroking the hundred-dollar bills ever so lightly. I felt like smoking a cigarette, an urge I had not had for thirty years.

I doubt if I can take it to the bank. How would I carry it anyway? In three brown Woollies bags? What about other customers? What about the teller?

I asked ChatGPT: "What happens if I take the money to the bank and put it into my account?"

It answered: "Depositing found money into your bank account without making any effort to find the rightful owner or notifying the authorities can have serious legal consequences."

Okay, forget that then. It must be whitewashed first. I must launder it.

I was surprised by how easily such thoughts came to me. I was now moving into true criminal terrain. Had I ever been there before? I looked back at my life. The last time I stole something was when I was four. A small, plastic, light blue toy-telephone from a friend of my sister. Oh no, wait. When I was fourteen or so, I stole books from a bookstore once. I thought my hippie father would find this amusing. So, I told him. He was furious. I never did it again.

"It's never too late," I said, stupidly.

What do you mean by that? It's never too late for what?

Stealing.

Technically, I've not stolen it.

Yes, you have.

The most remarkable thing about the whole situation was the absence of any feeling. I did not feel guilt, nor did I feel excitement. A vague dread lingered in the background; it had to do with what I should do with the money. It could not stay there on the table.

Why not?

Okay, it can stay there for a while, I suppose.

I fetched a tablecloth and spread it on top of the money. It looked bad. It looked exactly like a tablecloth with heaps of money underneath.

What about a sheet of heavy vinyl?

I googled: "heavy vinyl tablecloth." There was a Mexican store that had nice colourful, old-skool stuff. I ordered two meters of red flowers with black hearts on a white background.

Coffee!

I lifted the tablecloth, took a hundred-dollar bill and stuffed it in my purse.

"Red, come."

They tolerate dogs at Coolamon Café. As long as you stay out-side on the terrace. I ordered a flat white.

"Sorry, I only got a hundred-dollar bill."

"No problem," said the girl behind the counter and gave me the change.

My first money laundering offence.

I tried to feel something but felt nothing. Was I a psychopath? Or a sociopath? Was my true nature finally revealed? I smiled. The coffee was very good. To launder the whole pile like this was crazy. The volume of bills would increase tremendously. There would be coins. A vinyl sheet would not hold it down. Then I had an idea. I had lived in Japan for ten years in the 1980s, and Japan was still vividly alive in me.

The Japanese kotatsu!

A kotatsu is a traditional Japanese piece of furniture that consists of a low wooden table frame covered by a futon, or heavy blanket, upon which another tabletop sits. Underneath the table is a heat source, historically a charcoal brazier but now more commonly an electric heater. The purpose of a kotatsu is to provide warmth during the colder months. People sit on the floor with their legs tucked under the table and the futon draped over them, trapping the heat. The removable tabletop allows the futon to be securely positioned and provides a surface for eating, drinking, or other activities. The kotatsu is a staple in many Japanese households and is especially popular in the winter. It is often associated with family gatherings and cozy, communal living spaces. The primary use of a kotatsu is to keep warm during the cold seasons. It serves as a dining table, a work-space, and a place for socialising. The concept of the kotatsu dates back to the Muromachi period (14th century) in Japan, evolving from earlier designs that used charcoal braziers for heat. The modern electric kotatsu became popular in the mid-20th century.

There was no reason why this clever kotatsu concept could not be applied to my dinner table.

After I had walked Red at the clay pans, I went home briefly to measure the tabletop, then to Bunnings. I left Red in the yard. An hour later, I was sandpapering the rims of my second tabletop. When they were smooth, I placed the wooden top over the hundred-dollar bills and covered it with the tablecloth. Not perfect, but it would do for now. I could attach walls to the four sides later, so that the top became a box of sorts, while the volume of money grew through laundering.

What a pain in the ass.

During the days that followed, I learned to live with the loot. The Mexican vinyl tablecloth arrived. Its cheerful design gave my living room a lift, and my mood. I was obsessed with going back to The Spot to see if there was more money in the tree but resisted the urge. When I needed to shop, I used the money from the table, but I did not need much. I had taken one more bill from the table. The change of two hundred dollars was making my purse bulge. I hadn't handled cash since the beginning of Covid four years ago. Would the bank get curious if the spending from my accounts suddenly stopped completely?

What if I deposit small amounts? It's easier to leave it on the table. Think about it! I have enough cash for the rest of your life. What do I want then? I have everything I need. New things usually don't make me happy. The wheel of Samsara, you know? So why don't I take the loot to the police? I'm not ready yet. It's the idea. The idea of having money. The idea of having cash. Cash is not the same as money. Cash is, in a way, useless. This is hilarious. Real money isn't worth the paper it is printed on. Virtual, unreal money is worth its value while it does not exist. Very funny!

I figured that some of the money could be deposited into my accounts without raising suspicion. I decided to do a test and take the remaining money and some more in my purse to the bank. I deposited three hundred and eighty dollars and seventy cents.

A considerable dent you made there.

I laughed aloud: "Ha ha ha!"

Buy something you really want. Think about it. Something you've wanted for a long time. A Tesla.

I checked some auto sites. I would have to wait until a Tesla became available second hand in Australia, it seemed. Buying a new one with cash would likely raise suspicion.

I went to Harvey Norman and bought a light blue KitchenAid, placed it on the kitchen bench and looked at it. Although I was a good cook, I had been eating delivered take-away for years. I had once decided that I had done enough kitchen work for a lifetime and had stuck to it. Did I now have to start cooking again because I was suddenly rich? This seemed crazy.

A chef then. Someone who comes in once a week or so.

Let me think about it.

5

Day 14: Greed

On day fourteen, I went back to The Spot and, lo and behold, the man was there. I did not stop but drove past. My heart beating in my throat, I decided to do a drive-by every day or so from then on. He must live nearby because there was no car. But then, there aren't any houses there.

Is he a swagger, perhaps?

He had been standing in approximately the same spot as before, wearing a hat and sunglasses and a checkered shirt with the sleeves cut off. Maybe he had chosen that very spot to camp out at. Or maybe he was the owner of the cash. In that case, why had he hidden it? Had he stolen it and been facing similar dilemmas as I now had to deal with? After having walked Red, I sat at the table, elbows on the flowery vinyl, chin resting on my hands, thinking. I wasn't getting much done of the other things I was engaged in. My PhD research had come to a screeching halt, my sonnet writing had diminished to almost zero, and the business I was building was awaiting my attention. I looked at the light blue Kitchen Aid. It was a beautiful machine, but it was something I had wanted in the past. Somehow it had never made it into my possession somehow. It was now just standing there gathering dust and at a certain point I would have to put it away in the cupboard, just like the sewing machine and the overlocker. They were "just in case" things. Just in case I would start sewing again. Just in case I would start cooking again. Things of the past. I looked around my living room. There were the three Artemide balance-lamps that I had craved for so much during my early adulthood. One was on the antique meat safe, one on my desk, and one in the alcove. I still liked the design. The same counted for the red and yellow USA navy aluminium chairs and the leather Breuer chair. I had a thing with chairs for some reason. The rest of the furniture was a mishmash of old things. I liked it that way, I did not like matching things. My house was a cozy cave, perfect for my usual pursuits: my PhD research, my business, a start-up publishing house, and my writing. I usually moved from one piece of furniture to another to give my back a break from being in one position; I spent an hour on my bed to write my daily sonnet, or more sonnets if they came readily. I then moved on to the sofa, which was covered in colourful pieces of fabric, to read or edit a manuscript. Then on to a chair at the table. And so on. I usually ended my day in the yellow armchair with my feet on its ottoman, answering emails. In bed again, I watched Netflix and reels on Facebook until deep in the night and then worked some more. This lifestyle suited me fine.

What about travelling?

I realised I was done travelling. I had been everywhere, man. I'd lived and worked in the Netherlands, Belgium, Japan, Indigenous Australia and white-fella Australia and I had travelled extensively through Europe and Japan in my younger years. I had seen every continent and every museum along the way. I had a vague wish to go back to Japan. I had lived there in the nineteen eighties during the Economic Bubble and had witnessed that bubble burst. Japan had been the highlight of my life, ten glorious years. I frequently dreamed about it now, more than thirty years later. And that was exactly why I should not go back. Although one could buy a house in Japan nowadays for twenty thousand dollars. There were more than ten million empty properties in Japan, because Japan's population was shrinking at an alarming rate.

Why?

Japan's fertility rate was one of the lowest in the world, with an average of one point tree children per woman, far below the replacement level of the two point one needed to maintain a stable population. This decline was influenced by economic insecurity, high costs of living, and cultural norms that place heavy child-rearing responsibilities on women. Japanese women preferred to work. Japan had one of the highest life expectancies in the world, and a significant portion of its population was elderly. More than one-third of the population was aged sixty-five or older. This contributed to a higher death rate compared to the birth rate, further accelerating population decline. This demographic shift placed a strain on the economy and social services, as fewer working-age people were available to support the growing number of retirees. Economic stagnation and financial pressures made it difficult for young people to afford having children. High living costs, especially in urban areas, and the pressure to prioritise work over family due to Japan's intense work culture discourage family formation and childbearing. There was a lack of sufficient support systems for working parents, such as affordable childcare and equal parental leave. While the Japanese government had introduced various measures to counter the declining birth rate, including financial incentives for families, these had not been sufficient to reverse the trend. Efforts such as increasing the child allowance and providing more support for childcare had had limited impact due to the deep-rooted economic and social issues that needed to be addressed.

What once had been a feverishly urgent dream, a traditional house in the Japanese countryside, could now be bought easily and cheaply, even by a gaijin. It was probably too late in my life to do it, but I would keep it in the back of my mind.

You should write these things down. Make a list.

I opened my laptop. *A house in the Japanese countryside*, I wrote. I saved the document as *Wishes*.

When we see sudden wealth in movies, at least in the West, it usually results in alcohol and drug-fuelled partying with loud music and many beautiful people. Since I was old, I was not interested in beautiful people and the sex that came from it. Alcohol and drugs I had left behind me decades ago. I had never given them a thought after they had voluntarily left me. The whole image of new wealth disgusted me. It always had. *Nouveau riche* was a term of abuse in Europe. I tried to imagine what the Muslim's collective dream of wealth would be, but I had no clue. Buddhists would probably start a monastery with the money. Christian churches would probably fund a paedophilia ring under the cover of a charity with a name like *The Little Children Are Sacred*.

6

Day 16: Uncertainty

Why don't you start an Instagram account about the money? Hm, interesting, but too dangerous at present. People would try to find me.

I added *Instagram* to my list and dwelled for a while on what kind of photos and videos I could post. Me in my bath, covered in hundred-dollar bills. Me throwing the money around in my living room.

How cliché!

Me burning hundred-dollar bills one by one. Me eating hundred-dollar bills. Me shredding hundred-dollar bills with an office shredder....

Potential!

I added *Evil* to the word *Instagram*. *Evil Instagram*. It would easily gather millions of followers. If people made money putting their disabled children on display, then burning stolen money would do the trick too. I could earn tons of more money. I laughed. I made myself a coffee. Should I buy a good coffee machine? But that would rob me of the chance to go outside and experience the world, see a friend. The only reason why I went out was for coffee. My shopping was delivered weekly since the Covid lockdowns. I had not missed going to a supermarket since. This feeling was reinforced by my recent visit to a supermarket to spend some cash. What dreadful places they were! Light and loud and full of germs. I could now afford to shop at the health food store, but I dreaded the holier-than-thou atmosphere there. The local IGA seemed the best solution to burn some cash. Not too big and rather expensive.

Eventually, I got sick of just sitting there thinking. I texted my friend Penny and asked her if she felt like a cup of coffee somewhere.

"The coffee is really good at Coolamon at the moment. New barista."

Penny and I were the Coffee Gestapo; we constantly exchanged info about the quality of the coffee in the cafes around town.

"Okay, see you there."

For one crazy moment, I thought of telling Penny about the money.

Rule number one: don't tell anybody. Ever.

While driving to Coolamon Café, it occurred to me that I could not even give the cash away. I thought of my children in Europe. They were better off than I had ever been. Who did I know that really needed cash? Nobody, really. I knew of people who needed cash. I made a note on my list on my iPhone: *Charity?*

I did not particularly like the money going to people. People never had enough money. They spent it before they thought about it.

They always need more.

There was, in fact, only one charity that I liked in town: the Animal Shelter. I could perhaps drop off a couple of thousand dollars there. They had cages for abandoned and found animals at the beginning of their driveway. I could leave a sizable anonymous donation there in a box. I could monitor the cage, sitting in my car, unseen, until the box was taken by a worker and not a customer.

"You are very quiet," said Penny.

"Oh, am I, sorry. I was thinking of the animal shelter."

"Is everything alright with you?"

"Yes, excellent."

Think of something to talk about. You haven't thought of anything else but the money for weeks.

I drank my coffee while listening to Penny telling me about her drawing group, her choir… I felt quite disconnected.

Is this the price one pays for having money? Having cash is not the same as having money. Having money is much better.

"What would you do if you had a lot of money?" I asked Penny.

She thought about it. I observed her silently. We had known each other forever. Her once red hair had turned white. She still wore it plaited on both sides of her head, like a child. She had become even thinner than she had been. Dark spots on her pale skin had joined her freckles. She had long fingers with which she liked to drum on tables. She was doing that now, producing short burst of sound with one hand: Tururum tururum.

"Gosh," she said. "I don't know. Why do you ask? Have you received an inheritance? Are you contemplating giving it to the animal shelter?"

"No," I said, "I wish."

Tururum tururum.

"I think I would buy a nice house at the coast. I love the sea."

Tururum tururum.

"How much would that cost nowadays?"

Tururum tururum.

"Depends on were. A million, a million and a half… five million, the sky is the limit. Google realestate.com."

Tururum tururum.

"Since Google and AI, you cannot really ask questions in conversations anymore. I think only older people like us still do."

"Yes."

After our coffee, I did a quick drive-by. The man was at The Spot! He was looking for something on the ground. It was very likely the money belonged to him, even more likely that he too had stolen it.

I haven't stolen it.

Yes, you have.

I did not slow down but tried to take a picture of him while driving. At home, I enhanced the photo in Photoshop. It was not someone I knew. If he had stolen the money, from whom had he stolen it? I had not seen anything in the media regarding a bank robbery or theft. I had heard, years ago, that a group of kids had stolen a couple of hundred thousand from a well-known business-man in town. He had kept the money in a safe that was bolted to the floor. They had taken the safe, which was huge. Such is the nature of crime in this town. Kids were still breaking in, ramraiding buildings, joyriding in stolen cars… some as young as eight. All these kids were Aboriginal. Sad. It was better to leave the money hidden in plain sight. Nobody had ever come past Red anyway. Red was a racist. He went nuts when a blackfella came near. I had not taught him that. I stared listlessly at my list:

Tesla
Chef
Travel? Where?
House in Japanese countryside
Evil Instagram?
Charity > Animal Shelter

Although it was all within my reach, nothing of it felt real.

7

Day 18: Numbness

It was eighteen days since I'd found the cash, and I still didn't feel anything. I was waiting for a feeling to arise. Guilt, happiness, disgust, greed, sadness, regret, anything. Instead, a neutral veil seemed to have descended upon me. It was not something one could react to. I first needed a feeling to know how to move forward, so, I decided to dust off my meditation and mindfulness skills. I had once been a teacher of it but had taken my skills off the mat into the world a long time ago and had never looked back. Instead of a cushion on the floor, I used a chair. Vipassana seemed the best technique.

Vipassana meditation is one of the oldest forms of meditation that originated in India. It was supposedly rediscovered by Gotama the Buddha, and they say it has been preserved in its original form to the present day. Vipassana means "to see things as they really are," and the practice is centred around cultivating an awareness and understanding of the true nature of reality. Its primary goal is to purify the mind and eliminate mental impurities, such as anger, greed, and ignorance. By doing so, practitioners aim to achieve a state of equanimity and inner peace. It involves observing bodily sensations and the breath without attachment or aversion. Practitioners maintain a mindful awareness of their thoughts, emotions, and physical sensations, observing them without judgment. The practice begins with focusing on the natural breath to sharpen concentration. Once concentration is developed, practitioners perform a systematic body scan, observing sensations throughout the body in a specific order. Vipassana is a non-sectarian practice and does not involve rituals, rites, or prayers. It is taught in a way that is accessible to people of all backgrounds and religions. Vipassana is typically taught in ten-day residential courses, where participants adhere to a strict schedule of meditation and noble silence. These courses are offered with no charges for participation, accommodation, or food; they are funded by donations from previous students. I had done many of them. I had donated for even more. Regular practice of Vipassana meditation has been associated with numerous benefits, including reduced stress and anxiety, increased emotional regulation, improved focus and concentration, and a greater sense of overall well-being. Vipassana has spread worldwide, with meditation centres in many countries. It has gained popularity for its straightforward approach and profound impact on mental health and personal development.

I set my alarm for twenty minutes, closed my eyes, and began observing my breath. There were no thoughts. My head was a silent valley through which the wind of my breath blew freely. When the alarm went off, I reset it and began scanning my body. I started with my feet. There was a tinkling feeling in them. Probably the onset of diabetes. I never went to doctors, so I was ignoring it. I realised I did not mind if I died. I had done everything I had wanted to do and seen everything I had wanted to see. I simply had no wishes left.

I was not suicidal, far from it, but I was okay with anything that would happen from now, including death.

As I concentrated on the inside of my feet, they grew warm., then hot Ah, I was still able to do that! I moved my attention to my lower legs. What came to mind was that they were two cylinders full of stuff. There was no room for anything else in there, not for a soul, not for a feeling, not for a "me." Somehow, I was not "in" these lower legs. They were glowing nicely when my attention left them. I moved my attention to my knees. They were quite bewildering at first in their complexity. A Swiss army knife came to mind. I couldn't get my head around them and moved on to my upper legs. There was some pain there, deep inside the stuff that was in there. I breathed deeply, sending the wind of the breath into the legs, so to speak, and the pain disappeared. Ha, I could still do that too.

I scanned my whole body like that but found no feeling. Even my heart area and my head were completely empty of emotions. There were bodily feelings like pain, tingling, tightness, itch...but no emotions such as sadness, happiness, frustration...nothing! Had finding the money made me numb? Or was it because I was older? I had not the slightest idea what was going on. Maybe journalling would bring clarity? I opened my laptop and wrote a quick sonnet to warm up:

One Million Seventy-Nine Thousand One Hundred Dollars

I found one million seventy-nine thousand
one hundred dollars in the trunk of a tree
Fountains of hundred-dollar bills, mountains!
Enough for a two-year-long shopping spree
The problem is where to safely stash
it if one cannot take it to the bank

and one cannot. It needs to remain cash
Am I a thief now? No? Whom do I thank?
The problem is that I don't need a thing
I was content before the find occurred
by chance. I don't like cars; I don't like bling
The whole situation is rather absurd
It causes many moral dilemmas
That can only be solved by math's lemmas

I wasn't very happy with the last sentence, but nothing else came to mind. I'd fix it later.

I began the journal. I wrote:

I was not far from town, walking my dog, Red, in a nondescript piece of arid land next to the road leading to Hermannsburg. "Walking the dog" is an overstatement. I was sitting in the car while Red explored a piece of nondescript dirt at the side of the road. It was too hot to walk a dog that day. Going out had been a mistake. There was not a soul around. I had stopped the car and opened the door for Red. He had run into the patch of arid land that ended abruptly against the steep, red, rocky wall of West MacDonnell Ranges. There were rocks strewn everywhere, small trees, mulga scrubs and one big gum tree. Everything was shimmering in the stark afternoon light. I felt bored. Red peed against the white trunk of the ghost gum and then took a dump in the shade of its canopy. He looked ridiculous; staring into space while the turds left his bum. He stretched his whole body before he began to feverishly move his hind legs to bury the load he'd just lost. I laughed soundlessly. I expected him to return to the car, but there was something on the ground that demanded his attention. I called him.

"Red, come here!"

This seemed a good way of systematically dealing with the problem.

Ah, it is officially a problem now.

Suddenly irritated with myself, I grabbed a handful of hundred-dollar bills from the kotatsu, drove to Hervey Norman and began pacing the aisles to see if there was something I desired. Nothing. I drove to Exotic, an expensive furniture shop, and tried again. Nothing. I hated being in shops. I hadn't shopped in shops for years. The few things I needed or desired I bought online. Back home, I window-shopped dresses, shoes, and bags online. But I had enough dresses and shoes. I had one handbag that I really liked and didn't want more.

I'm not a consumer anymore.

There were nineteen Teslas for sale in Australia suddenly. None of the owners accepted cheques. Cheques were passé. I realised that to own a Tesla, I needed a garage. There were too many kids out there stealing or damaging cars at night. I called a builder and asked if they would accept cash or cheques. They didn't.

Viva the electronic economy!

I'm not a consumer anymore. This was a thought-statement that deserved some further soul searching. In contemporary society, it seemed to me, identity is increasingly shaped by consumerism. This shift was a marked departure from the ways identities were historically constructed, where one's sense of self was rooted in factors such as occupation, social class, community roles, and cultural heritage. Historically, identity was closely tied to one's role within the community and one's contributions to society. In agrarian societies, people were identified by their familial roles and their work. A person might have been known as a farmer, blacksmith, or weaver, with these roles not only defining their livelihood but also their place in the social structure. Community ties were strong, and ipeoples' identities were a collective reflection of their societal contributions and relationships. During the Industrial Revolution, identities began to shift, but still remained largely tied to one's occupation and class. The rise of urban centres and factory work meant that people were increasingly identified by their roles within the industrial economy. Social class remained a marker of identity, influencing where one lived, the social circles they moved in, and their overall lifestyle. Cultural heritage and tradition also played a critical role in shaping identity. Religious beliefs, local customs, and ancestral traditions provided a framework within which individuals understood themselves and their place in the world. These identities were interwoven with the fabric of daily life and community, offering a sense of continuity and belonging. The mid-20th century, around when I was born, saw the advent of mass consumerism, a phenomenon that has transformed how people construct their identities. Post-World War II economic booms and bubbles, coupled with the rise of advertising and mass media, encouraged people to see themselves as consumers first and foremost. This shift was further propelled by the advent of credit. Today, identity is heavily influenced by consumption patterns. People are often defined by the brands they wear, the gadgets they own, and the lifestyles they portray on social media. The rise of digital culture has only amplified this trend, with platforms like Instagram and Facebook allowing individuals to curate and display their identities through the products they consume. Advertising plays a crucial role in shaping consumer identities. It not only promotes products but also sells lifestyles and ideals. Companies use marketing techniques to create aspirational images, linking their products to notions of success, beauty, and happiness. As a result, people strive to emulate these ideals, seeking validation and identity through their consumption choices. The use of luxury goods as status symbols is a clear indication of how consumption has become a key marker of identity. The constant demand for new products fuelled unsustainable consumption patterns, leading to resource depletion and environmental degradation. It exacerbated social inequalities, as those who cannot afford to consume at a certain level felt marginalised or inadequate.

Being old has several advantages when it came to identity. A woman becomes invisible after a certain age, which feels like a liberation to many, because women are primarily judged by their physical appearance when they are young. I, for example, did no longer give a single fuck about what others thought of my appearance or behaviour. Zero. Nix. Nada. Nil. I did what I wanted to do. I wore pearls while driving an old Toyota HiAce and socks in sandals under a dress. For some reason, doing what I want required little money. Trying to pump myself up to a consumer again may proof futile.

Still, I'm holding on to that money a little longer.

8

Day 20: Coming Up for Air

I had been dreadfully unproductive since I found the money. My PhD research needed urgent attention and my publishing house was stagnant. I had not written a word, except for my list. I looked at my pathetic wish list again.

Tesla
Chef
Travel? Where?
House in Japanese countryside
Evil Instagram?
Charity > Animal Shelter

I already employed a cleaner and a lady who did my ironing. That was enough people to deal with in my life. I crossed out Chef. I would wait until AI came up with a household robot. How difficult could it be? I did not want AI to do my writing, I enjoyed my writing. I wanted AI to do my dishes! I decided that, from today onwards, I would dine only in restaurants. I don't know why it took me nearly a month to figure that one out. I loved dining out and hated cleaning up after cooking. I drove to Tali and ordered a three-course lunch. Carpaccio, beef cheek with Paris mash, and pistachio ice cream for dessert. I had an icy-cold glass of dry white wine. Coffee. Brandy. Delish. I paid cash and drove myself home for a well-deserved food-overdose nap. It was the first time I had enjoyed the money. When I was young, I could never eat alone. But now I enjoyed it. I liked being alone in general. I liked the silence in my head and dreaded the noise other people made. I loved the tranquillity of being alone, the serenity of true solitude, the calm quietness, removed from the multitudes. I loved being uncommunicative. Muteness, yes, it suited me right to the core. The absence of any collaboration was what I most adored. Come, get out into the sunshine, they said. Let's cycle and swim and do gymnastics! However, I said: Hey, who are you to tell me what to do. I don't tell you: Write a book, or a poem, start a business or follow a course; Hey, get off your high health-horse.

It was time for a drive-by. I decided to talk to the man if he was there. I had Red with me as a pretext and for protection. I had boots on this time. The man was at The Spot! The boots made walking towards him much easier.

"Hi," I said, while Red ran off to do his thing.

"Hi."

He looked at me longer than was polite, although it was hard to tell. He was wearing his sunglasses. So was I. Did he remember me from the first encounter when I had pretended to check my tyres?

"You're not supposed to walk a dog here."

I feigned I did not know. "Oh really?"

"It's National Park. The West MacDonnell Ranges."

"Oh. Sorry... Don't you have a dog then?"

In other words: what are you doing here?

"Nah. I've lost something here, I think."

"What have you lost?"

He hesitated. "Something personal."

My heart was pounding hard. "I'm sorry to hear that."

"Yeah," he said vaguely, stuffing his hands in the pockets of his jeans.

"Want me to help you look for it?"

"Nah. But thanks anyway."

"Put a notice on the Alice Springs Bulletin Board," I suggested.

"What's that?"

"On Facebook," I clarified.

"Don't do social media."

"I can do it for you."

Clever move.

"Nah, I'm good."

"Shall I give you my number, in case you change your mind?"

"Nah, I'm good."

He is the owner of the money. Definitely. Or the thief of it. He's "good".

"You need a ride into town?"

"Nah, I'm good."

"Have a good afternoon then."

"Yeah, you too."

I called Red. My heart was thumping heavily.

He definitely is the man. Is he suspecting me? And if so, what then?

Giving him my phone number would have been stupid, I realised. He might have figured out where I lived. He might have come looking for the money. It was better to cease the drive-by for a bit. I'd never seen him before. I'd been in town for twenty-five years. I knew plenty of people.

This town has twenty-four thousand inhabitants.

He was in his mid-thirties. Some kind of tradie. Muscled. No accent. A typical Australian toxic bloke. Jeans. Belt. Boots. RM Williams shirt with the sleeves cut off. Akubra hat. Ray-Ban sunglasses. No jewellery. Generic as hell. Not a talker. I pitied his wife if he had one. I doubted that he was gay. Anyway, I had to stay away from him. I should not attract his attention in any way. It was strange that he had no car with him. What did that even mean?

It occurred to me that he might have a family. In that case he could use the money. But I somehow doubted it. If he was a family man, he'd have a car with him. It was abnormal to be out there without a car. It was at least an hour and a half walk from town. Who goes walking three hours to find something "personal"? If one knew what that "something personal" was, one would better understand. But a man with kids would not have three hours to spare at the drop of a hat. Then it occurred to me.

He's a drug dealer. Someone drops him off and picks him up to look for the money. They're in it together. This made him dangerous for sure.

Having solved this puzzle, I lightened up considerably. If it was drug-money, I did not feel an obligation to give it back.

Wait. Did you say "feel"?

I seemed to be able to feel after all. This considerable cheered me up too. I grabbed a hundred-dollar bill or two and went to The Feast, where I ordered eggplant in tomato sauce, pork belly with rice and a lavender panna cotta. A glass of white wine. Coffee with cognac. Satisfaction guaranteed! They were expensive, the size of the panna cotta ridiculous for its price, but I did not need to worry about that. If I changed my attitude to certain things I would be fine with the money hidden in plain sight. I decided to not lock my door even when out, like before the Big Find. Wasn't this what experts recommended to those that won the lottery, to not change anything?

In the parking lot I spotted Johan, our local homeless guy. There were many homeless people in town, but Johan was well known. He would sit quietly and observantly in café's, in churches, in parking lots and food courts, wearing a three-piece suit from Vinnies, a floppy hat that had seen better days and a grey canvas riding coat. He possessed a bicycle and a swag. Well organised, polite and clean, he kept to himself. He was the town's model homeless teddy bear. Everyone liked him. Many had unsuccessfully tried to home him. Luckily, he had ceased his branching out into flute playing in front of supermarkets. It had not been a success for obvious reasons, he could not play and seemed extremely tone-deaf. I stuffed a fifty dollar note in his hand and wished him a good afternoon. Discretely keeping Johan fed and dressed was the least I could do.

9

Day 24: The Disappearance of Cash from Society

I had always been a great fan of anything digital, but I had to rethink some of that to come to terms with the fact that my life revolved around cash now. In recent years, the use of cash had been steadily declining, supplanted by digital payment methods such as credit cards, mobile payments, and cryptocurrencies. While the shift towards a cashless society offered several conveniences, it also raised significant concerns. One of the most drawbacks seemed the loss of privacy. Cash transactions are inherently private and leave no digital trail, thereby allowing people to conduct transactions without surveillance. Digital transactions are recorded and can be monitored by banks, governments, and corporations. This increased visibility raised concerns about the potential misuse of personal data, such as unauthorised tracking of spending habits and financial profiling. The transition to a cashless society can also marginalise certain segments of the population, particularly those who are unbanked or underbanked, like Johan A quick google search revealed that, according to the World Bank, around one point seven billion adults globally did not have access to a bank account. These people relied heavily on cash for their daily transactions. The elimination of cash would create significant barriers for them, barriers that I now fully understood, exacerbating financial exclusion and inequality. Elderly people and those in rural areas struggle with the transition to digital payments due to a lack of technological proficiency or inadequate access to digital infrastructure. This was definitely the case where I lived. Our town was full of semi-literate people. Cash once was a universally accepted and straightforward form of payment that does not require technological literacy. It provided people with a sense of control over their finances. It allowed for budgeting in a straight-forward manner and could help prevent overspending. In a cashless society, the ease of making digital payments could lead to impulsive spending and financial mismanagement. Without the physical representation of money, people might find it harder to keep track of their expenditures. Relying solely on digital payment systems made people dependent on financial institutions and technology providers. This dependence was problematic in situations where there are technical failures, cyber-attacks, or outages. Cash served as a reliable fallback option in such scenarios. The disappearance of cash also had implications for economic stability. Cash played a critical role during times of crisis, such as natural disasters or economic downturns, when digital payment systems may be disrupted. In such situations, cash could serve as a lifeline, enabling essential transactions when other methods are unavailable. A cashless economy increased the risk of systemic vulnerabilities. Centralised digital payment systems were targets for cybercriminals, and a successful attack could paralyse the economy. Cashless transactions also widened the gap between rich and poor. For example, small businesses and informal sectors such as local markets often relied on cash transactions. These businesses faced increased costs associated with digital payment processing fees and the need to invest in new technologies. As a result, they struggled to compete with larger corporations that can more easily absorb these expenses. And cash played a cultural role in many societies. It was often used for gifting, tipping, and charitable donations. The disappearance of cash was leading to a decline in these practices.

I was happier, but still often felt overwhelmed by the cash on the table. When that happened, I lay on the floor. I just suddenly dropped. I called it "floor time". This practice provided a sense of grounding and physical relief, helping to calm my mind and body. Lying on the floor helped relax my muscles and relieve the tension the money caused. Physically connecting with the ground created a feeling of stability and calm. Taking a break from the cash reset my emotions and thoughts. After floor time I wrote in my journal.

I went to Bella Alice for lunch that day. I ordered a Mother Earth pizza with a white base, Mozzarella, fresh fior di latte cheese, aged parmesan, mushrooms and truffle oil. For dessert I chose a honey panna cotta. The dishes were strangely expensive. But then, who cared? An Italian waiter in an old-fashioned European suit served me.

"Voila, here's your pumpkin and eggplant salad, your garlic focaccia, your pannacotta al miele, and your tiramisu al caramello salato."

"Eh, I did not order that."

"Yes, you did."

"No, I didn't. And do you always bring the desert out at the start?"

"Now, don't you put this on me, lady, this is what you ordered."

"I don't want it."

"Well, that's your problem."

"Right." I stood up and walked to the door. The waiter blocked the door.

"What?"

"You haven't paid."

"I don't usually pay for things I did not order. But here, my chap, I'm in a good mood today." I stuffed a hundred-dollar bill in his hand. "Keep the change."

I slammed the door so hard that the windows rattled.

Back home, I wrote a review on the Alice Springs Bulletin Board:

Bella Alice. Overpriced Attitude. I order at Bella Alice. Somehow the order arrives completely wrong. I tell them immediately. They say: "This is your fault, don't put it on me" There's no will to help at all. Immediate aggression instead. $100 down the drain. Never again! One star.

After an hour there was a reply of owner:

Thank you for taking the time to share your thoughts about your recent experience with Bella Alice. As the owner, I genuinely appreciate hearing feedback from our customers, even when it highlights areas where we may need to improve. However, I couldn't help but notice a few intriguing aspects of your review that I felt compelled to address: Your use of vivid and dramatic language, such as "overpriced attitude" and "immediate aggression," certainly paints a colourful picture. It's almost as if a minor issue was transformed into a grand spectacle. You have quite the talent for storytelling! It's fascinating how a " Focaccia and a small salad that was never ordered somehow found their way onto your bill. While mistakes can happen, jumping to such firm conclusions without considering the possibility of an honest error seems a bit hasty, don't you think? The portrayal of our staff's "immediate aggression" is quite the tale. It's remarkable how one-sided a story can become when only one perspective is presented. Perhaps a more balanced approach would lend greater credibility to the narrative. Your review is a masterpiece of negativity, curiously devoid of any mention of positive aspects. If one were to examine a broader collection of your reviews, would they discover a recurring theme of dissatisfaction and conflict? It's just a thought that crossed my mind. It's always enlightening to observe customers opting for public platforms or groups (especially those they administer and direct) to air their grievances, rather than seeking a direct resolution. The approach undoubtedly garners attention – public shaming can be so much more gratifying than engaging in private discussions, can't it? Constructive criticism is often the catalyst for business improvement, yet your review seems to lack any suggestions or balanced feedback. One might wonder if the intention was to harm rather than to help. How intriguing.

We sincerely value every customer's opinion, even when it's delivered with such unbridled passion. Should you ever wish to discuss your concerns in a more balanced and constructive manner, we are always here to listen and strive for improvement. However, we cannot help but question the true purpose of a review like this, especially when it's shared publicly on a group that you own and administer, reaching a significant portion of the Alice Springs community.

Best regards, Giuseppe, Bella Alice Owner

After this reply, I needed floor-time again. Lots of it. *Bloody European pricks!* I kept thinking, which was strange, because I was European myself. Well, I was Australian now, but for forty-five long years

I had been European. But maybe being Dutch did not count on the scale of European food quality. The Netherlands had a dreadful food history but had caught up nicely in recent years with culinary fashions such as fusion. Just like England, really. I found Italians unbearable. I had shared a house with one. Ah, house sharing. Another thing I never had to do again! On and on my thoughts raced....

Overpriced Pretention' your name should be! A good name for an Italian restaurant. They should park a burning bicycle between your balls!

Why do I even care?

Yes, why?

10

Day 31: Memories of Poverty

My cleaning lady Julliette came.

"You've got a new tablecloth," she said. "Nice. Cheerful."

"Yeah, thanks, don't remove it, I keep some cash underneath it," I said.

"No problem."

She'd never look now.

"I'm going out to drop off my ironing," I said, thereby indicating that I trusted her completely.

"See you later," she said.

I dropped off the laundry basket at the door.

"You're paying cash. Nice!" said the ironing lady, Natasha.

"Is that better?"

"Of course," she said.

"Why?"

"Oh, you know..."

The black economy still exists.

I started thinking about this. Hiding cash from the ATO. Small businesses did it to survive. I'd done it. I wasn't used to thinking like a person with cash yet. I was still thinking like a person needing cash.

I returned home only twenty minutes later and could tell the table-cloth hadn't been moved. This hiding in plain sight was working. Julie was mopping the floors.

"Would you prefer to be paid cash?"

"Yes, of course," she said.

"Okay, from next time on then."

"Cool."

I now had a little list with points where I could pay or donate cash.

Juliette
Natasha
Johan
Animal Shelter

After Juliette and Natasha, I needed some floor time. I closed my eyes. I was back in my childhood. I began reintegrating feelings that I had lost touch with, aspects of my personality that I had lost touch with. It was as if I were a car losing pieces as it drove down the road. There was a trail of pieces of myself that I had left behind. Now all those pieces came back. An avalanche of memories came at me, not only memories of events but memories of feelings, of ways of being, ways to relate to myself and the world, as a tone of the here and now that I used to know as a child, and I had lost touch with. There was a memory of being poor. As a small child my needs were barely met, although I always had shoes and enough food. This changed when I was eleven. I experienced hunger then. The circumstances did not matter. I remembered the feeling of being hungry and how it consumed me entirely. For a while I ate from other people's fridges. Was I stealing from them? I didn't remember whether the food was given or not. When I was a young teenager, this situation continued. I left school at fourteen and learned to work for money. The first years I spent all my money on food. I was very afraid of being hungry again. It occurred to me how foreign this was in todays' world, in the parts where I had lived anyway. Had this really happened to me? Yes. I tried to look at the girl I then was. But I could not get out of my first-person view memory. I wanted to sooth her. But I could not see myself. I could only feel the pain of being hungry, the obsession with food. The feeling of things not being sufficient.

The situation had repeated itself when my children were very young. I remembered going through pockets to find the last cash we had. This had instilled a great fear of poverty in me. This fear had driven me most of my life. Why then was I not feeling much around the money? Should I not be hugely relieved? I thought about samsara.

Samsara, in Buddhism, refers to the cycle of birth, death, and rebirth that all beings undergo. The cycle is characterised by suffering and is driven by karma and ignorance. Understanding it is crucial for the pursuit of enlightenment. Ignorance, or not understanding the true nature of reality, keeps one trapped in samsara, misunderstanding the nature of the self and clinging to a false sense of identity. Overcoming ignorance through wisdom and insight is essential for liberation from samsara. The goal is to break free from samsara and achieve nirvana. The Wheel of Life is a visual representation of samsara. At the centre of the wheel are the three poisons: ignorance (delusion), attachment (desire), and aversion (hatred). Greed is one of the primary defilements that perpetuate the cycle of birth, death, and rebirth; a form of attachment and craving, which is seen as a root cause of suffering and a significant obstacle to achieving enlightenment. Greed arises from a desire for material possessions, sensual pleasures, and certain states of mind or experiences. This leads to attachment, where one clings to these desires, believing they are essential for happiness and fulfilment. Greed is often intertwined with other defilements, such as ignorance and aversion. One of the antidotes to greed is the practice of generosity.

Voila, there was my answer. I tried to remember what Christianity had to say about samsara and greed.

The Bible foolishly did not address the concept of samsara. Samsara was a concept from cyclic religions like Hinduism, Buddhism, and Jainism. The Bible frequently warned against greed, viewing it as a sin that leads to spiritual and moral decay.

1 Timothy 6:10 states:

> For the love of money is a root of all kinds of evil. Some people, eager for money, have wandered from the faith and pierced themselves with many griefs.

Luke 12:15:

> Then he said to them, 'Watch out! Be on your guard against all kinds of greed; life does not consist in an abundance of possessions.'

The Bible encouraged believers to find contentment and not to seek fulfilment in material wealth.

Philippians 4:11-12:

> I am not saying this because I am in need, for I have learned to be content whatever the circumstances. I know what it is to be in need, and I know what it is to have plenty. I have learned the

secret of being content in any and every situation, whether well fed or hungry, whether living in plenty or in want.

Acts 20:35:

> *In everything I did, I showed you that by this kind of hard work we must help the weak, remembering the words the Lord Jesus himself said: 'It is more blessed to give than to receive.'*

2 Corinthians 9:7:

> *Each of you should give what you have decided in your heart to give, not reluctantly or under compulsion, for God loves a cheerful giver.*

I preferred to think about my newly acquired wealth in Buddhist terms. Or was there a non-religious way of thinking I could turn to?

In Stoicism, wealth and greed are addressed with a focus on virtue, self-control, and rationality. Stoics categorise wealth as an "indifferent," meaning it is neither good nor bad in itself. What matters is how one uses and relates to wealth. They emphasise that virtue is the only true good, and external things like wealth are secondary and should not control one's happiness or moral integrity. Seneca wrote extensively on the topic of wealth. He argued that wealth should be used wisely and ethically, and that one's moral character should not depend on material possessions. In Letters he states: "It is not the man who has too little, but the man who craves more, that is poor."

Epictetus taught that desires for external things, including wealth, can lead to disturbances and unhappiness. He advised focusing on what is within one's control—namely, one's own actions and attitudes. "

Marcus Aurelius advised simplicity and self-sufficiency. In *Meditations* he reflects on the transient nature of wealth and the importance of focusing on inner virtues: "Very little is needed to make a happy life; it is all within yourself."

Aristotle spoke on the ethical use of wealth. He taught the "golden mean," the virtuous balance between excess and deficiency. He believed that wealth should be used to achieve higher, virtuous ends, rather than being an end in itself.

Epicurus addressed wealth and greed with a focus on simple pleasures and the avoidance of pain. He argued that the pursuit of unnecessary wealth leads to anxiety and dissatisfaction. Instead, Epicurus advised seeking contentment through simple, natural pleasures and friendship.

Thoreau echoed similar sentiments. In Walden, He explores the idea of living simply and eschewing unnecessary materialism: "Wealth is the ability to fully experience life."

11

Day 32: Cranky Old Bird

I had fallen asleep on the floor. I woke up in a dream. I was in a former relationship. My partner was angry. Something to do with money. An LP was playing loud on the stereo. Eurythmics.

Sweet dreams are made of this
Who am I to disagree?
I travelled the world and the seven seas
Everybody's looking for something
Some of them want to use you
Some of them want to get used by you
Some of them want to abuse you
Some of them want to be abused

I woke up from the dream, sat up and shook my head. Why did I know that song by heart in my dream? How could I wake up in a dream? Then I remembered the money. Was that a dream too? I took a couple of hundred-dollar bills from the kotatsu. They felt real in my hand. Not a dream.

With the song still pounding in my head, I dressed up and drove to Hanuman for dinner.

It was pleasantly busy in Hanuman. There were several people I knew. Some invited me at their table, but I declined and chose a table in a quiet corner. The trumpet mushrooms topped with pork and crab mince, spices and coconut cream were succulent and spicy. I had them with a dry white wine that lasted over the main course of red snapper and the dessert of Shrilankan love cake; a semolina cake baked with cashews, crystalised ginger, honey, rosewater, cardamom & nutmeg. Then a cup of tea. I leaned back in my chair contently between every course and listened to the buzz of voices talking. I had become rather seclusive since I found the money. My life was about money, food and death now. Like the movies of Juzo Itami. Would that ever change again? I did not know. I did not want to know. I bought food with the money. I enjoyed it. I would be separated from the money by death. Simple as that. I spent some time after dinner thinking about a succession plan for the money. I had to rewrite my will. But how? Whom did I love most in the world? This was an interesting question. I noticed that I loved those that were near me the most. Friends. My love was conditional though. If they would start being annoying or demanding, it was easy to love them less. My kids. Oh yes, I had loved them fiercely, but they were nearly old men now and they were far away. I did not know the grandkids well enough to truly love them. I loved them like I loved most children. I noticed that I was quite alone but that this did not bother me. We are alone when we are born and when we die. Alone seemed the natural state. Even with friends, we mainly talked to ourselves. Years ago, I would have denied that; would have disliked this thought. I believed in helping others back then. Now, I found those that helped others annoying. What they actually did was disempowering others. Show others they knew or did better. The only clean way to help others was by giving them money. Money brought freedom. Did it?

I was definitely turning into a cranky old bird. I did not show it. I paid the dinner, smiled at the waiter and put some coins in the staff jar. I'd never been able and therefore not willing to do so. It felt good. People in hospitality earned ridiculously little, just like nurses and preschool teachers. Disgusting really. They had the most important jobs of all. I put some more coins in the jar and left. Johan was sitting in the hallway of the hotel where Hanuman was located. I gave him a fifty.

He said: "God bless you."

"And you," I chirped.

I felt like skipping to the car. I tried to but noticed that I could not skip any longer. When had I lost the ability to skip, I wondered. The body going that way; clumsy and stuffed. I did not like it. Maybe I should start weightlifting. No yoga for me anymore! Yoga teacher were hidden helpers. I did not want to be helped. I wanted authentic raw experiences. Yoga had been hijacked by commerce. Like so many once-good things. We consumed yoga now, wearing hemp active ware. We'd stolen it from the Indians. It had happened to art too. Nearly all my friends were consumers of art. There were far too many artists. This brought the quality down.

In the car, Juzo Itami came to mind again. There was an element of sex in his movies too. Food, Death, Money and Sex. I remembered the scene were lovers exchanged a raw egg yolk between their opened mouths. In what movie was that again?

12

Day 40: Effective Altruism

I had made a list of organisations in town that needed money. Going through it made me ill. Most of the town was Catholic. There was no way I was going to give money to a Catholic or even a Christian organisation. I hated the way they treated the poor. The food and clothes they gave were of terrible quality. I'd seen the Christmas presents they gave. Cheap shampoo and plastic hairbrushes for women and polyester socks and beanies for men. I had to look further afield. I checked out effective altruism but found it cultish and fashionable. Sam Harris was promoting it. I gave him the benefit of the doubt. I investigated it a bit further.

Effective altruism turned out to be a real philosophy and social movement, mainly found in Silicon Valley and New York, that uses evidence and reasoning to determine the most effective ways to benefit others. It focused on using one's resources to do the most good, guided by careful consideration and analysis. This approach involved comparing the cost-effectiveness of different charitable interventions and choosing those that provide the greatest benefit per dollar. It encouraged one to consider global issues and solutions that might offer the most substantial positive impact. It was not about giving for the sake of giving; it was about ensuring that each act of generosity was as impactful as possible. Central was the idea that we should focus on problems that are significant, tractable, and neglected. It often prioritised global health initiatives, such as distributing anti-malarial bed nets or deworming treatments, because these interventions were cost-effective and save many lives. It supported efforts to alleviate extreme poverty, reduce animal suffering, and mitigate existential risks like climate change and future pandemics. It encouraged one to think about one's careers and lifestyle choices. This idea was known as "earning to give."

The movement was not without its criticisms and potential pitfalls. Examining the darker aspects revealed an interplay of ethical dilemmas, practical challenges, and unintended consequences. Things might bite back. The emphasis on maximising utility could lead to morally questionable decisions. It could lead to a form of ethical myopia, where the ends justify the means, potentially resulting in actions that are dehumanising or disrespectful to those being helped. Its reliance on data and measurable outcomes could marginalise important but less quantifiable aspects of human well-being. It was an elitist culture where voices from less privileged backgrounds were marginalised. The concept of "earning to give," raised ethical concerns. It could perpetuate and even exacerbate systemic inequalities by legitimising and supporting industries that contributed to social and environmental harm. For instance, an person working in a high-paying but ethically questionable industry, such as fossil fuels or tobacco, might donate a substantial portion of their income to effective charities. While their donations may do good, the net effect of their career choice could still be negative, undermining the very principles of effective altruism. Another dark aspect was the potential for burnout and disillusionment among its adherents. The movement's rigorous standards and high expectations could create pressure on people to constantly seek the most effective ways to do good. The intense focus on effectiveness could overshadow the intrinsic value of altruism, reducing acts of kindness to mere calculations rather than expressions of genuine compassion. The global focus of effective altruism seemed to neglect local needs and undermine the importance of community-based solutions. The global outlook could lead to a form of moral relativism where the immediate needs of local communities are deprioritised. This could weaken social bonds and reduce the sense of solidarity and mutual support that is crucial for resilient communities.

One of the prominent figures associated with ethe movement was Peter Singer, an Australian moral philosopher whose work has significantly shaped the movement. Singer's book *The Life You Can Save* outlined argument for why individuals in affluent countries have a moral obligation to help those in extreme poverty. Singer himself practiced what he preached, donating a substantial portion of his income to highly effective charities.

Another influential advocate was Dustin Moskovitz, co-founder of Facebook and Asana. Along with his wife Cari Tuna, Moskovitz founded Good Ventures, which collaborated closely with the charity evaluator GiveWell to identify and support the most effective charitable causes. Good Ventures had donated millions of dollars to initiatives that address global health and poverty, animal welfare, and biosecurity.

Elie Hassenfeld and Holden Karnofsky, co-founders of GiveWell, were also central figures in the movement. GiveWell conducted research to identify charities that deliver the most cost-effective interventions.

Tech entrepreneur Sam Bankman-Fried was another advocate. As the founder of the cryptocurrency exchange FTX, he had pledged to donate a significant portion of his wealth to high-impact causes.

Bill Gates, while not exclusively an effective altruist, aligned closely with many of the movement's principles through his work with the Bill & Melinda Gates Foundation. The foundation focused on addressing some of the world's most pressing issues, such as global health, poverty, and education.

Julia Wise and Jeff Kaufman committed to donating a substantial portion of their income to effective charities. They shared their experiences through their blog, *The Giving Gladly*, inspiring others to consider how they could make a meaningful difference through their philanthropic choices.

I decided this line of action was not for me. I liked to keep things local.

13

Day 45: In Plain Sight

I never locked my house or car. Even in this crime ridden town. Or rather because of it. The thought behind this was that if some-one wants to get in, they would regardless, and they'll cause damage while doing so. I'd been leaving my house open for more than forty years. When I was in my early twenties, a large, black, Bakelite radio had been taken from the windowsill in my kitchen and another radio, not dissimilar to it but beige, had been put in its place. I'd never unravelled that mystery.

My car window had been broken not too long ago when I had accidentally locked my Toyota HiAce bus. Since the culprits are very young in this town, I now store books for them in the back. I had special bookshelves built and picked up second-hand children's books at lawn sales. Not one book had ever been taken yet. I imagined what would happen if some boisterous youths entered my cottage. They might overturn the table. I should secure the second tabletop. I lay on the floor to think about how to best do that. Tablecloth clamps would do the trick. They would hold the two tops together. But they may snap sideways if the table fell. Holes with screw and nuts would be better but would make getting to the cash out daily more difficult. Glue clamps would be too bulky and visible... ropes too inconvenient... In the end I left it as it was. I took the tablecloth off the table, then the second tabletop and smoothed the stash out. I'd been taking bills from the rims. Dents had formed there. I filled these up with bills from the middle.

I tried to get passionate about the money again. Have strong feelings. What did I really care about? Women's homelessness? Hungry children? Animal going extinct? Human trafficking? War? Climate change? Refugees in camps? Elephants killed for ivory? These conditions caused feelings of anger in me, sadness and disgust with the human race, like they did in anyone else with a pulse, but the sheer endlessness of these problems caused an immediate numbing as well. I had to go to an affected place in the world to have real feelings. But I was too old to travel that way. The thought alone made me want to weep. Environmental organisations in town made me cringe with vicarious embarrassment over their obligatory woke slogans while they could not even keep their own small gardens thriving.

14

Day 51: Fed Up

I was laying on the floor. Never in my life had I been so exhausted. Was it the money? Or was I sick? I had to rule out the latter if I wanted to know for sure. I grabbed my iPhone from the floor and made an appointment with my doctor. My doctor referred me to the hospital. I loved the local hospital. It had saved my life twice. The doctors and nurses were from all possible continents. Treatment was free for locals. Over the next few days, I had all tests one could think of done and left with a clean bill of health.

So.

The money was causing the exhaustion. It had isolated me, made me lethargic, made me fearful, confused, greedy, overwhelmed, uncertain, numb and secretive and now it was making me tired. Okay, I had enjoyed a couple of nice meals...I had made Johan and the Animal Shelter happy, but I would be better off without the money.

Let that sink in.

The next question was: how did I get rid of it?

Call the police, duhuh.

If I called the police, should I admit that I had ironed the money? That I had taken bits and pieces of it? This seemed a major pain in the neck. What would the volume be like now? To determine the volume of $1,079,100 in Australian $100 bills, I'd need to measure one bill. I did so with an old ruler. The dimensions were approximately: 15.8 cm x 7.0 cm x 0.013 cm. I wrote. I did a quick calculation on paper.

$$\text{Number of \$100 bills} = \frac{1,079,100}{100} = 10,791$$

$$\text{Volume of one \$100 bill} = \text{Length} \times \text{Width} \times \text{Thickness} \quad \text{Volume of one \$100 bill} = 15.8 \text{ cm} \times 7.0 \text{ cm} \times 0.013 \text{ cm} = 1.4374 \text{ cm}^3$$

$$\text{Total volume} = 10,791 \times 1.4374 \, cm3 = 15,497.67 \, cm3 \, \text{Total volume} = 10,791 \times 1.4374 \text{ cm}^3 = 15,497.67 \text{ cm}^3 \text{Total volume} = 10,791 \times 1.4374 \, cm3 = 15,497.67 \, cm3$$

The total volume of $1,079,100 in Australian $100 bills was approximately 15,497.67 cubic centimetres. To determine if this fit in a weekend bag, I compared it with the typical capacity of a weekend bag (20,000 to 30,000 cubic centimetres). Since 15,497.67 cubic centimetres is within the range of a standard weekend bag capacity, $1,079,100 would fit comfortably in a standard weekend bag. Feeling like a criminal, I took a black weekend bag and made it dirty in the garden. I poured water over it and stamped on it while it was sitting in mud. When it was dry, I pulled the colourful Mexican tablecloth away from the table and took off the top blank wooden tabletop. A sea of bright green hit me. I stacked the money in the bag and rang the police. Half an hour later two officers arrived. A man and a woman. They looked like children to me.

"I found money," I said and opened the bag that was sitting on the table.

They both took a step backwards. The female produced a note-pad while the male proceeded to take photos of the bag. The female asked the obvious questions. When? Where? How?

"How much is it?"

"I don't know."

I lied like I had never lied before. "While walking the dog, I found the bag yesterday at the claypans hidden under a bush."

They took the bag with them.

"What happens if you don't find the owner?" I asked.

"We'll let you know."

It was clear they had no clue what the protocol was, so I told them.

"The protocols for handling found money and returning it to the finder if the owner cannot be located is as follows: You must record the details of the find, including the amount, location, and circumstances under which the money was found. Then make reasonable efforts to locate the rightful owner. This may involve checking missing property reports, and public notices. The police will hold the money for ninety days. If the owner is not found, it may be classified as unclaimed property. You will then assess whether the money can be returned to me. You will provide a process for me to submit a claim, which involves completing a claim form. I sign a receipt to acknowledge the return of the money. In certain situations, if the money is suspected to be connected to criminal activity or if there are other legal implications, different procedures may apply."

They were standing before me like two puppies, listening. I sighed with relief when they departed. They put the bag on the back seat of the police car. Would they steal it? Divide the loot between them? They drove off. I waved.

Bye.

I took the second tabletop and the Mexican tablecloth to the shed. Then the cleaning lady came and said: "Hey you have gotten rid of that nice tablecloth."

"I got sick of it pretty quickly," I said. Then I remembered I had promised to pay her in cash from now onwards.

"I have to go to the ATM," I said. "See you a bit later."

The ATM was broken. I grinned. Even after the money had gone it caused me grief.

I texted Penny. "There's a new café on Todd Street. They claim to have the best coffee in town. Wanna try?"

"Sure."

"CU in 30."

The coffee at the new place was indeed very good. It was hand-brewed in two glass balls. There was an unusual fruity aroma to it.

"I like it."

"It's still early days."

"True. Let's see how they go."

"I found a huge amount of money," I told Penny. Sticking to the story I told police; it was good to talk about it. Back home I immediately resumed my normal activities of research for my PhD and building my publishing house.

15

Ninety Days of Peace

For ninety days I did not think about the money. I slipped into my old life seamlessly. In the morning, I quickly made my bed and stepped outside. Shadows of dreams were still lingering while I looked at the sky while stretching my arms out to the endless blue that was still pale but would soon blaze. I drank a quick can of coffee and called Red for a walk through the neighbourhood while it was still cool. The shadows were still long, and everything shimmered in the early sunlight. Birds were chattering everywhere. One sounded like a tune by Charlie Parker: tadatadada dada. I looked at the fences and houses of my broken town, now and then saying hello to a fellow dog owner. Red was relentless in his pursuit of places to lift his leg. He nearly pulled me off my feet. I watched how the pavement rolled by as I walked. I let boredom wash over me taking a deep breath.

When we arrived home it was already getting hot. I fed Red, changed his water bowl and filled the bird baths. The trees in the garden were causing dark and golden patches to fall all over me and I bathed in the sensation of light and shadow. The water in the bird-baths was made of diamond.

Once inside, I watered the plants while talking to them.

"Yes, you too suffered when the money was here." I could sense it."

I sat down with my laptop for a breakfast of sourdough dark rye with butter and more coffee, fresh this time. By noon I had written a couple of paragraphs for my thesis. Every word counted and I had to go over it many times to get it right. The citations took forever. Then all was put in Calibri twelve, double spaced for the texts' body and ten single spaced for the footnotes. A young bird was picking at my kitchen window. It had been doing that for a year.

I looked around the room and approved of it. Nothing needed changing. I liked the way my shoes were lined up at the door, a habit that had survived from Japan, the way the light fell on the old barn door that was my table. I stretched again and ate something small for lunch, a piece of bread with hot tomato, salt and garlic perhaps and a glass of milk. It was amazing how little I needed to be content.

The afternoons, I spent doing what is now called 'creative writing'. I hated the term 'creative' and called it simply 'writing'. My world was about letters, words and sentences since I had retired. It was a world I belonged in. I had begun writing about the cash and tried to remember how it had made me feel. One afternoon I remembered the stash in the bed post. I went to look at it. it was still there of course. A reminder of a heaviness, complexity, and chaos. I quickly put the lid on the bedpost.

It was wonderfully silent in my cottage, hardly any traffic noise ever reached it. The bird sounds died down around five. I ordered my dinner on Menulog, because I dreaded cleaning up after cooking eating w. I ate while lying on the sofa with my laptop. Then I took Red for a ride and a walk and looked at the sunset and how people went about their ways at dusk in our town. The light quickly faded, nightfall came quickly, and when the coolness descended, I opened all windows to let in the fresh air and the eventide. The whole evening was dedicated to my business. I switched on a lamp or two. The yellow light gave me a cozy and homely feeling. I usually worked until twelve midnight or longer. The radio was on; RN was whispering in the background or ABC Classic if I had to concentrate. Insects buzzed against the fly screens and geckos gathered on the glass. A pale moon rose. Dingos were howling in the distance. I listened to an audio book to get myself to sleep, usually something mind-bending about the nature of reality. I went through several emotions during the day, between my various tasks, I had thoughts that were soothing or caused painful emotions. I gently moved from mild happiness to mild sadness and back. The days were all the same and perfect. They were like word-studded diamonds, while my dreams were like shadows. They balanced perfectly. Sad moods were connected to the past, happy tempers were connected to the future. Sometimes I was mad. But all emotions and feelings were mild and passed by like the weather and nothing stuck to me. I was free of them. I never stepped in the same river twice. I was free.

16

Day 130: Hello Darkness, My Old Friend

After ninety days, the money was returned to me. I signed a form at the police station and walked to the car with the dirty bulging bag. Some people stared. I didn't care. While driving home I thought about how I now needed to learn to live with the money like one must have to learn to live with an ex after one decides to, after all, not leave the relationship and marry and have a kid instead. Things were easier now because the money was legitimately mine. I was sort of married to it and pregnant. Of possibilities presumably. I could put it in the bank. What I was going to do with it I had no clue. The past ninety days had been perfect. But maybe that had been a reverse honeymoon phase, just like the freedom after the separation from the ex-now-spouse.

At home I opened the bag a stared at the green mass.

"Hello Darkness, my old friend," I said. "I've come to talk with you again."

The money did not talk back. I called the bank.

"I must deposit a lot of cash. How do I go about that?"

"How much are we talking about?" a female voice spoke.

"More than a million."

It was silent for a while on the other end. "Hang on, I put you on hold."

After a couple of minutes of torturous music, a male voice spoke: "I understand you need to deposit a considerable sum?"

"Yes."

"How much?"

"I'm not sure it needs to be counted. It's more than a million in hundred-dollar bills."

"We should make an appointment," the man said. He was clearly Indian. "How about tomorrow at eleven a.m.?"

"Perfect. Who do I ask for?"

"Peter."

"Alright Peter," see you then.

At the bank I was treated like royalty. Peter was waiting for me at the door and ushered me through a side door to a private office. He was impeccably dressed, an exception for this town. A grey suit over crisp white. A tie even. He was indeed Indian and I doubted his real name was Peter, yet his business card said Peter Kumar. He was pleasantly soft spoken and well mannered. I put the dirty bag on the desk, and he did not even flinch. Instead, he made a call ordering coffee and cake.

"You will have to sign a form and explain where the money came from," he said apologetically.

"Yes, that's fine."

"I will fill it out for you. You just have to date and sign."

I had never been treated like this before in a bank. Usually, I stood in line for an hour and filled out forms on the narrow counter, balancing bags, dropping pens and having to go to the toilet badly.

The coffee arrived. The cake clearly came from the bakery a couple of doors down the street. Peter took his time pouring the coffee and serving the cake. His hands worked industriously.

"Sugar?"

"Milk?"

A woman came to take away the bag.

The chair I leaned back into was very comfortable and pleasing to the eye. Peter now produced the form and smoothed it in front of him on the table.

I could hear a counting machine in a nearby room rattling through the one-hundred-dollar bills.

"How did you obtain the money?" Peter asked after we'd gone through the usual details.

"I found it."

He did not even blink. Very professional. I smiled. He smiled. I handed him the copy of the release form of the police. He clearly had never seen one, but pretended he did.

"More coffee and cake?"

"Yes, please."

I sipped my coffee while Peter filled out the form.

"How would you like to invest the money?"

"I don't know yet. Just put it in my savings account for now."

"Investment is key. We have several very profitable options."

"So why are you still working here?"

He looked at me baffled.

"If you have such goods deal, why are you not rich yet?" I clarified.

Peter smiled sourly. "Very well. Here is some information about investing with us and loans."

"Loans?"

"Yes, you can borrow quite a bit."

"Right."

Peter opened the door for me, and I stood outside with a handful of flyers. Rich-ish. Banks give you an umbrella when the sun shines and take it away when it rains. I realised how true this was.

Investing.

Once home, I leafed through the investment flyers that Peter had given me. I decided, as usual, to carve my own path. I decided to see how Bitcoin worked. I went to BTC Markets dot net.

BTC Markets was one of Australia's most prominent cryptocurrency exchanges. The platform had earned a reputation for providing a secure, reliable, and user-friendly environment for trading digital assets. It was known for adhering to regulatory standards and industry best practices. Compared to other platforms, I found, they offered relatively low trading fees, which could help maximise returns. They also promised robust customer support through a help centre, email support, and active social media channels. However, during onboarding, I immediately got tangled in a maddening identification loop. I gave up after about an hour and moved on to CoinSpot dot com dot au.

Coin Spot aimed providing a straightforward and secure way to engage with cryptocurrencies. At its inception, the platform focused on simplifying the process of buying and selling digital assets, addressing the growing interest in cryptocurrencies like Bitcoin and Ethereum. Over the years, Coin Spot had expanded its offerings and user base, reflecting the increasing popularity and acceptance of cryptocurrencies in Australia. They had played a significant role in the adoption and growth of cryptocurrencies in Australia. Its onboarding process was easy and before I knew it, I had one thousand dollars in my Bitcoin wallet. That made 0.0100525 BTC.

This was enough excitement for a day. I went to Casa Nostra for some Australianised Italian food enjoyed in bad acoustics. Dining there with a friend was nearly unbearable, but while alone the racket caused a pleasant white noise. The interior was extremely retro, red and white checkered tablecloths, distasteful wooden chairs, old tourism posters and plastic palms. Or maybe the plants were real, who cared? It was the kind of place where plastic looked like wood and wood looked like plastic. The restaurant was not licenced to serve alcohol. In such a setting one had to have the Bolo. It had far too much sauce, which I approved of. They had but one dessert: a killer vanilla slice, the best in town. The place was packed as usual. The collective voices thundered, and it was a hustle and bustle of waiters and waitresses from all over the world in beige aprons. The lighting was worse than the acoustics. After dinner, I checked the Spotcoin ap and had lost $11.80.

A dignified beginning.

I verified the value of Bitcoin over the past five years and the graph looked like a young mountain range, with steep, sharp mountains and rocky valleys. What was worth twenty thousand dollars ten years ago, was now worth over a hundred thousand. Whether that upward trend would continue, nobody knew. It was a bit like the pearl necklace and the house overlooking Central Park.

Once upon a time in New York city, a wealthy woman saw a double pearl necklace in a jewellery store. It cost one and a half million dollars. The woman owned a house overlooking Central Park worth about the same. She said to the jeweller:

"I want that necklace."

"Very well," said the jeweller, "I'll exchange it with you for your house."

"Deal."

That year a Japanese businessman discovered how to cultivate pearls using oyster farms. The value of the necklace fell to one hundred and twenty thousand dollars. The value of the house went up slowly but steadily.

Was Bitcoin the pearl necklace or the house?

17

Day 132: Sparkly Things

It was about time I researched the tax situation. One would think that once one had money, one could take it easy. This was not true. I had not done a thing about my thesis and my business. The perfect ninety days without the money seemed long ago.

I keyed figures into several calculators on the ATO website and found out that I was to pay forty five percent tax over the found money.

Let's fund some more coal mines, shall we?

I really needed an expert, but I was weary of financial experts because if they were that good why were they still working in the job? Even I knew that working in a job does not make you rich. So why were they not playing the stock market or whatever it is that rich people do instead of slaving away?

I had a vague idea of what I should do, I could donate to charitable causes, contribute to my superannuation, income average, form a trust, offset some small business losses and use deductions and offsets. I worked a couple of days on these options until the tax situation was slightly better.

I noticed that I did not really give a toss about paying taxes. There would be enough left.

I learned about the four times twenty-five rule: invest twenty-five per cent in buildings, twenty-five in gold or silver, twenty-five in crypto and twenty-five in stocks.

I bought a two-bedroom unit and put a tenant in it. That took two and a half months to accomplish and much miscommunication with real estate poodles. I spent much time in the cars of real estate agents, making meaningless conversation. It was crystal clear that they did not have my interest in mind but the buyer's. The concept of buyer's agents had not reached our town yet. Then there were the inspections. Clearly, the agents shared a bed with some inspectors and not others. I went against their recommendations just to prove my point. I used a pleasant older guy who the real estate agents quite hated because he pointed out too many defects to their liking. Then there was the interviewing of potential tenants. There was a shortage of housing, so I had many requests. I chose an older single female just because it was more difficult for them to remain housed. It turned out to be the right decision. Dora paid the rent in time and seemed the perfect tenant.

Next, I researched how to invest in silver. I liked silver better than gold. It sparkled better. Cooler.

Silver had a dual role as both a precious metal and an industrial commodity. Its price was influenced not only by investment demand but also by industrial demand in sectors like electronics, solar energy, and medical devices. This dual demand could lead to high volatility. It came in the form of bullion bars and coins. Storing and insuring these physical assets added an extra layer of responsibility and cost. Junk silver, comprising coins with high silver content but no numismatic value, offered another physical investment avenue. Knowing what a nuisance the paper money had been, I could only imagine the pain coins would bring. I preferred a more liquid and easily tradable option, such as silver exchange-traded funds. These funds hold physical silver or silver futures contracts and are traded on stock exchanges, providing exposure to silver's price movements without the need for physical storage. Examples include the iShares Silver Trust and Sprott Physical Silver Trust. Investing in silver mining stocks was out of the question, I did not want to contribute to mining in any way, so a basket of mining stocks was out of the question too.

Silver futures and options involved agreements to buy or sell silver at a predetermined price on a future date, while options contracts gave the right, but not the obligation, to transact silver at a specific price before a certain date. Both methods required a deep understanding of market dynamics and came with inherent risks. Silver certificates, issued by banks, represented ownership of a specific amount of silver, offering a convenient way to invest without the need for physical storage. Similarly, digital silver platforms like BullionVault or Goldmoney allowed investors to buy and hold silver in digital form, backed by physical silver stored in secure vaults. Mutual funds and index funds that had exposure to silver, either through physical holdings, futures, or mining stocks, provided additional investment avenues. These funds could track specific indices related to silver prices or silver mining companies, offering a yet more diversified approach. When investing in silver, it was important to consider market volatility, as silver prices could be unpredictable. Understanding the associated fees and transaction costs was also crucial. To embark on silver investment, thorough research seemed essential. Maybe it was better to buy gold instead?

Gold had long been considered a safe-haven asset, particularly during times of economic uncertainty and inflation. Its historical stability and recognition made it a trusted store of value. The market for gold seemed highly liquid, allowing for easy buying and selling. Gold's relatively high value per ounce made it more convenient to store and transport, requiring less storage space compared to silver. Gold prices tended to move more steadily than silver prices, providing a more stable investment. In times of economic downturns or high inflation, gold's safe-haven status tended to shine, attracting investors seeking security.

My first job, a long time ago, had been for Gassan Diamonds in Amsterdam. I looked at their website. I liked the blue diamond cut the best. I wasn't much into the Australian pink diamonds. Investing in diamonds came with several drawbacks. The diamond market was known for its lack of clarity. Prices could vary widely depending on factors like cut, clarity, colour, and carat, which were not always straightforward for non-experts to assess. Unlike gold, which had a well-defined market price at any given time, the valuation of diamonds was not as transparent. Diamonds are not as liquid as other investments like stocks or bonds. Selling quickly and without losing a significant portion of the investment was more challenging because it depended on finding a buyer who agrees on the diamond's value. The process of buying and selling involved high transaction costs, including commissions, fees, and significant markups from retailers, which could erode profit margins. The diamond market could be volatile too, influenced by changes in fashion trends, economic conditions, and mining outputs. Unlike other commodities, diamonds did not have a unified market index, making their price fluctuations less predictable. Unlike gold and silver, which were commodities that could be melted down and measured, each diamond was unique. This lack of standardisation made it difficult to create a uniform market price. Physical diamonds needed to be stored securely and insured, which incurred additional costs that could impact the overall returns from diamond investments. The mining and sale of diamonds had been linked to human rights abuses and environmental damage. Even with certifications like the Kimberley Process, there were still concerns about the sale of conflict diamonds and the impact of mining practices.

Too bad! No sparkly things for me.

18

Day 195: Perfect Days

I investigated stocks and bond and nearly fell off my chair with boredom. No matter how hard I tried, I could not concentrate on the task at hand. I looked out of the window for hours, reluctantly getting back to the dreaded subject. But, investing in stocks and bonds seemed a fundamental strategy and involved different levels of risk and potential returns that I needed to know about.

Stocks represented ownership shares in a company. When one bought stock, one became a shareholder, meaning one owned a portion of that company. Stocks were known for their potential to yield high returns compared to other forms of investment. If the company performed well, its stock value might increase, and one might receive dividends if the company distributes profits. Investing in stocks could be risky; stock prices were volatile and could fluctuate widely based on the company's performance, market conditions, and economic factors. There was also the potential for losing the entire investment if a company went bankrupt.

Bonds, on the other hand, were debt securities issued by entities such as governments, municipalities, or corporations. When one bought a bond, one was lending money to the issuer in exchange for periodic interest payments and the return of the bond's face value at maturity. Bonds generally offered lower returns compared to stocks but were considered safer investments. They provided a steady income stream through regular interest payments, known as coupon payments. While generally safer, bonds did carry risks such as credit risk (the issuer might default) and interest rate risk (rising interest rates could make existing bonds with lower rates less attractive, reducing their market value). There were government bonds which were considered very safe; municipal bonds, ssued by states, cities, or other local government entities, often tax-exempt and corporate bonds issued by companies, that were higher risk but also yielded higher interest rates than government bonds.

I had to decide how much risk I was willing to take. Stocks were suitable for a higher risk tolerance, whereas bonds are better for stability. I had to diversify my portfolio and not put all my investments in one asset class. A mix of stocks and bonds could help manage risk. I had to consider professional advice, especially because I was new to investing.

Who do I like enough to invest in? Who has enriched mu life? Starlink.

The satellite internet service developed by SpaceX, was not a separate publicly traded company. It remained a division of SpaceX, which itself was privately owned and not publicly traded. Therefore, I could not directly invest in Starlink as its own entity.

Apple then.

Investing in Apple Inc. proved a straightforward process. Reviewing their annual and quarterly reports, available on Apple's

Investor Relations website, provided valuable insights. I had to determine what I wanted to achieve with my investment in Apple. Was I looking for long-term growth, dividends, or short-term gains? My investment strategy should align with my risk tolerance.

Once my brokerage account was set up, I transferred funds into it. When I was ready to buy, I could place an order.

After purchasing the stock, I had to keep an eye on my investment. This included following monitoring Apple's performance, keeping tabs on market conditions, and staying informed about technological trends and economic factors that could affect Apple's business.

Apple paid a quarterly dividend.

It was important to regularly review my investment portfolio This involved adjusting my holdings in Apple based on performance, market conditions, or changes in your financial objectives.

I found this all extremely uninspiring, so I asked Peter at the bank to do it for me. Peter was delighted.

I could finally go back to my perfect days. On some perfect days, I drove Red and myself past the spot where I had found the money. Sometimes the man was there, and sometimes he was not. I never stopped to talk to him. I did not want him to spoil my perfect days. I did not want anything to ever spoil my perfect days again.

When an unexpected discovery disrupts a quiet life in the heart of the Australian Outback, an ordinary woman's world turns extraordinary. *Cash!* by Suzanne Visser is a gripping novella that delves into the moral complexities and emotional turbulence that follow the unearthing of a hidden fortune.

Accompanied by her dog, Red, our protagonist stumbles upon a tree trunk filled with rolls of hundred-dollar bills. What begins as a curious find quickly spirals into an exploration of greed, fear, and the burdens of sudden wealth. From cautious secrecy to wild fantasies of spending, she wrestles with ethical dilemmas and the practical challenges of living with—and potentially hiding—a massive sum of money.

Set against the stark, arid landscape of the West MacDonnell Ranges, *Cash!* offers a narrative filled with suspense and philosophical reflections. Visser masterfully crafts a story that is as thought-provoking as it is thrilling, leaving readers to ponder: *What would and should you do if you found a fortune?*

Suzanne Visser LLM (1957) began her writing career in the Netherlands. She published through several good publishing houses such as Atlas, Leopold and Bert Bakker. Her novel De Vismoorden; *The Fish Murders*, was translated into French, German, and Spanish. Clear Mind Press has published this successful book in English.

Visser has lived in Australia since 2000. She now writes in English. She is a versatile and productive writer.

Short stories:

De pracht van het dagelijks leven; Bert Bakker, 1991

Thriller:

De Vismoorden; Atlas Uitgeverij, 2000; published in German as Das Japanische Rätsel, DVA, 2001; in French as Les Meurtres au Poisson, Noir sur Blanc, 2002; in Spanish as Sushi, Ediciones B., 2003; in English as The Fish Murders, Clear Mind Press, 2022

Children's book:

De Verdwijning, Leopold, 2005

Novel:

Terra Nostra, Bookhost, 2003

Novel:

Een man met mooie benen, Mistral, 2006

Non-fiction:

I, Unborn, Undying (a Search for the Self), For a Clear Mind, 2016

Non-fiction:

The Elephant's Tooth, Crime in Alice Springs, Clear Mind Press 2022

The Elephant's Tooth, Crime in Rural Australia, Clear Mind Press 2022

Non-fiction:

Marks on Paper, Essays on drawing, seeing and looking, Clear Mind Press 2023

Non-fiction:

Never Retire, an exploration of old age, Clear Mind Press 2023

Non-fiction:

I, Myself and Me, Clear Mind Press, 2024.